I0813286

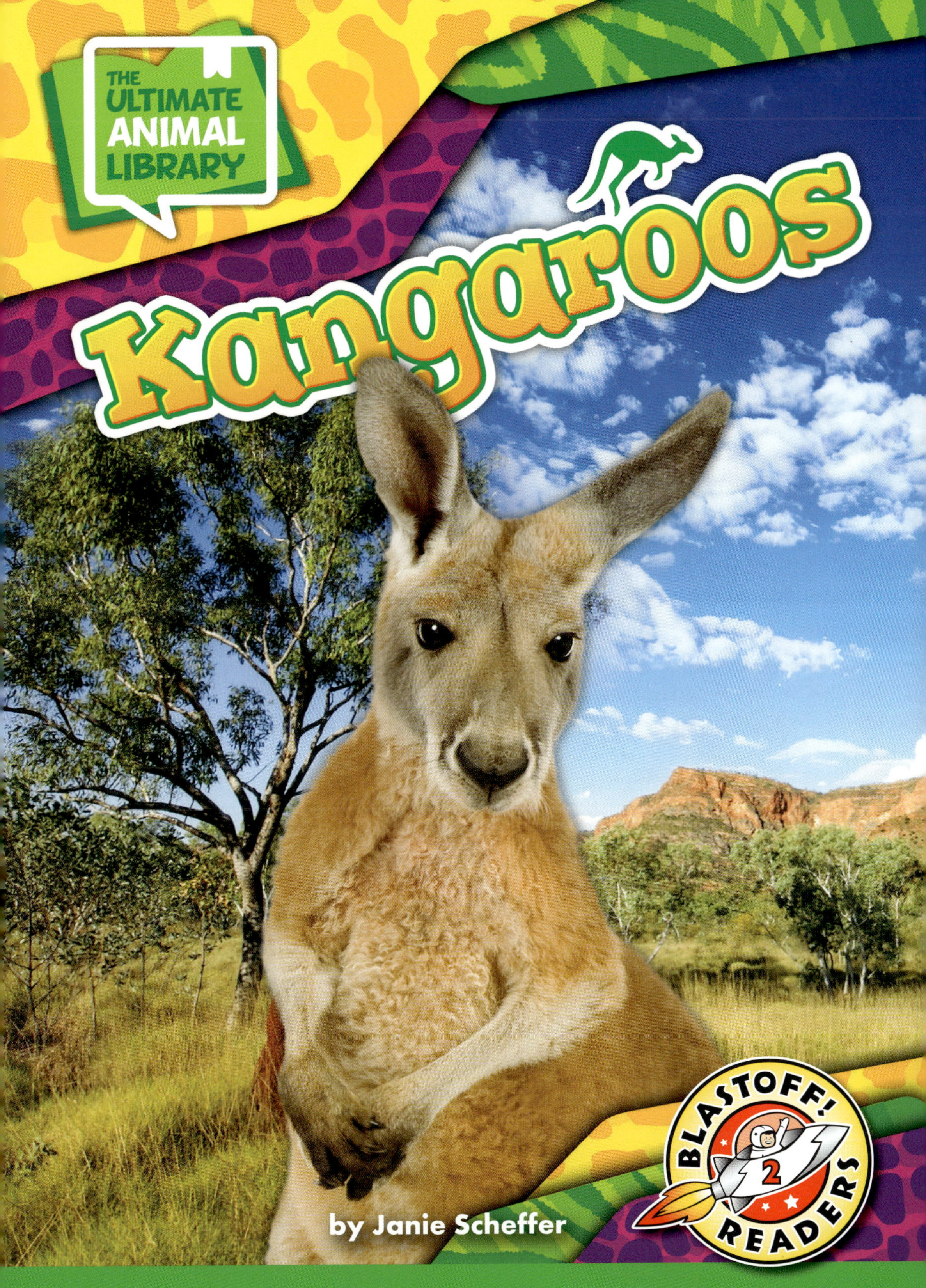

Kangaroos

by Janie Scheffer

BLASTOFF! READERS, AN IMPRINT OF BELLWETHER MEDIA BY FLUTTERBEE

Blastoff! Readers are carefully developed by literacy experts to build reading stamina and move students toward fluency by combining standards-based content with developmentally appropriate text.

Level 1 provides the most support through repetition of high-frequency words, light text, predictable sentence patterns, and strong visual support.

Level 2 offers early readers a bit more challenge through varied sentences, increased text load, and text-supportive special features.

Level 3 advances early-fluent readers toward fluency through increased text load, less reliance on photos, advancing concepts, longer sentences, and more complex special features.

★ **Blastoff! Universe**

Reading Level

Grade K → Grades 1–3 → Grade 4

This edition first published in 2026 by Bellwether Media, Inc.

For information regarding permission, write to Bellwether Media, Inc., Attention: Permissions Department, 3500 American Blvd W, Suite 150, Bloomington, MN 55431.

Library of Congress Cataloging-in-Publication Data is available at www.loc.gov or upon request from the publisher.

ISBN: 9798893047950 (hardcover)
ISBN: 9798893048957 (ebook)

Editor: Elizabeth Neuenfeldt   Designer: Brittany McIntosh

Printed in the United States of America, North Mankato, MN.

Table of Contents

What Are Kangaroos?	4
Life in Mobs	12
Growing Up	18
Glossary	22
To Learn More	23
Index	24

What Are Kangaroos?

Kangaroos are **marsupials**. Females carry their young in pouches on their bellies! There are a few kinds of kangaroos. They are mostly found in Australia.

Red Kangaroo Report

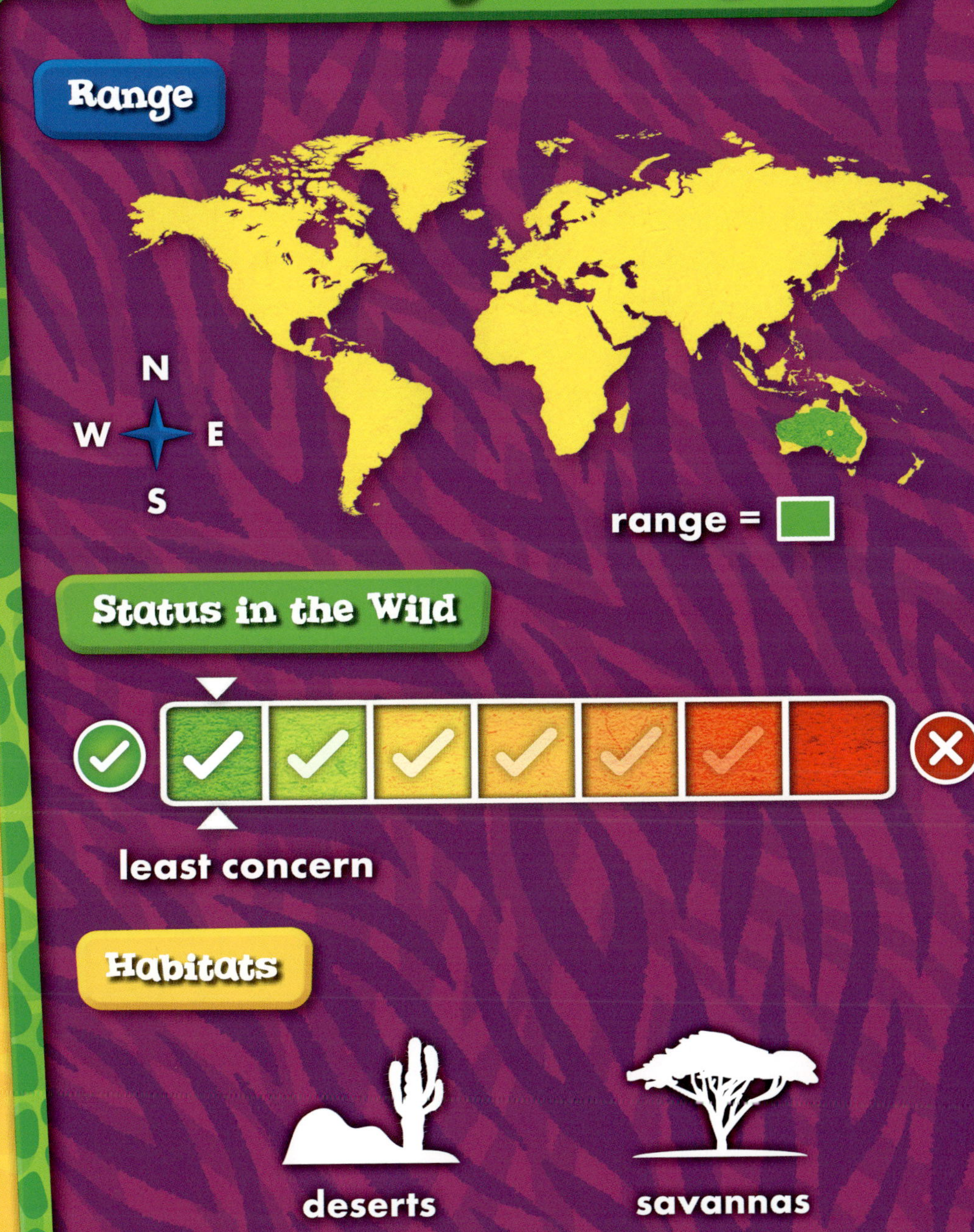

Kangaroos are the world's biggest marsupials!

Some are over 6 feet (2 meters) tall. They can weigh up to 200 pounds (91 kilograms).

Kangaroos leap quickly!
They have long, strong legs.
Their feet are big.

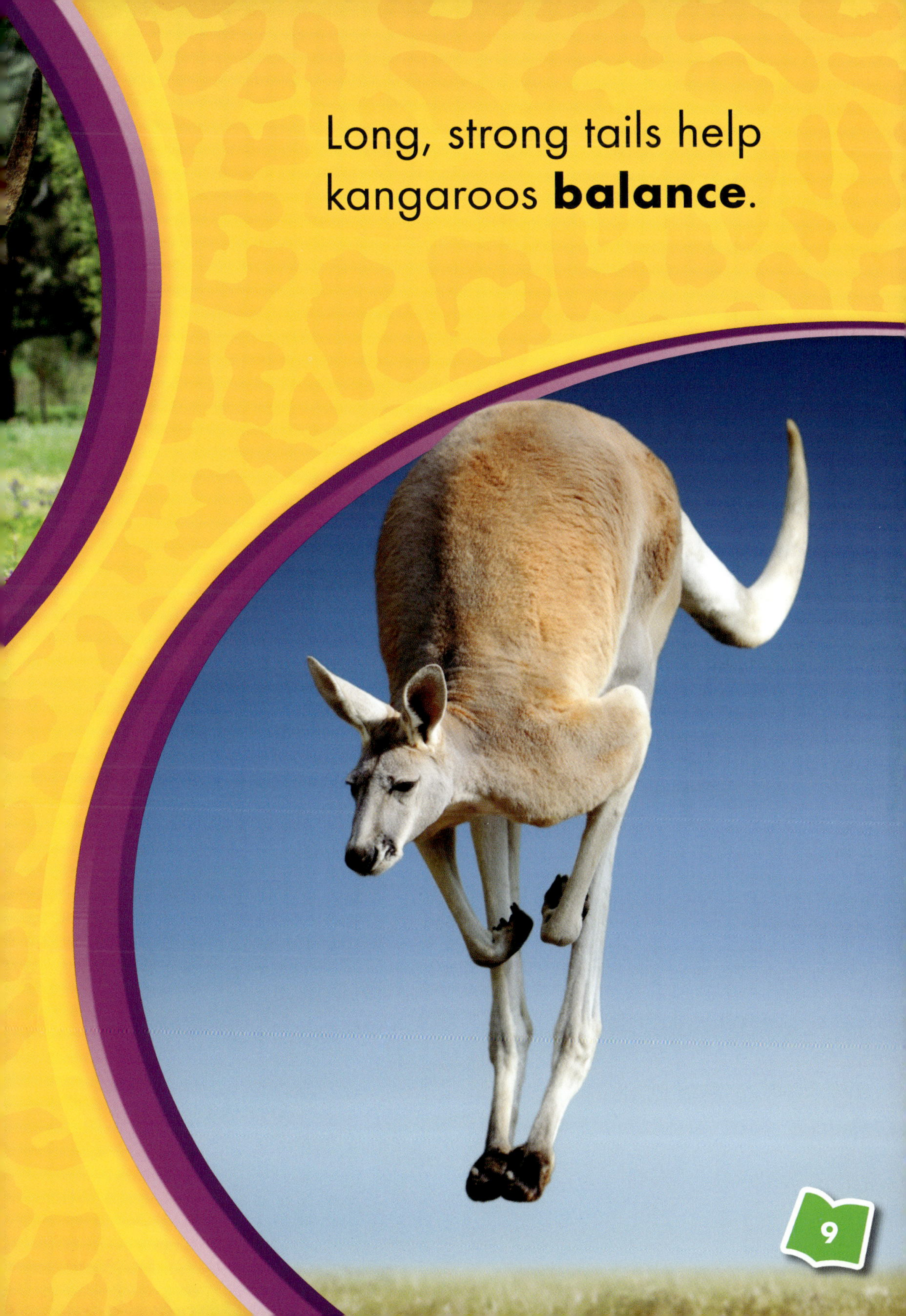

Long, strong tails help kangaroos **balance**.

Kangaroos have small heads with big, round ears. Their ears can turn.

They have sharp claws on their hands and feet.

Spot a Kangaroo
big, round ears
long, strong tail
long, strong legs

Life in Mobs

Kangaroos often live in hot **deserts** and **savannas**. They rest in the shade during the day to stay cool.

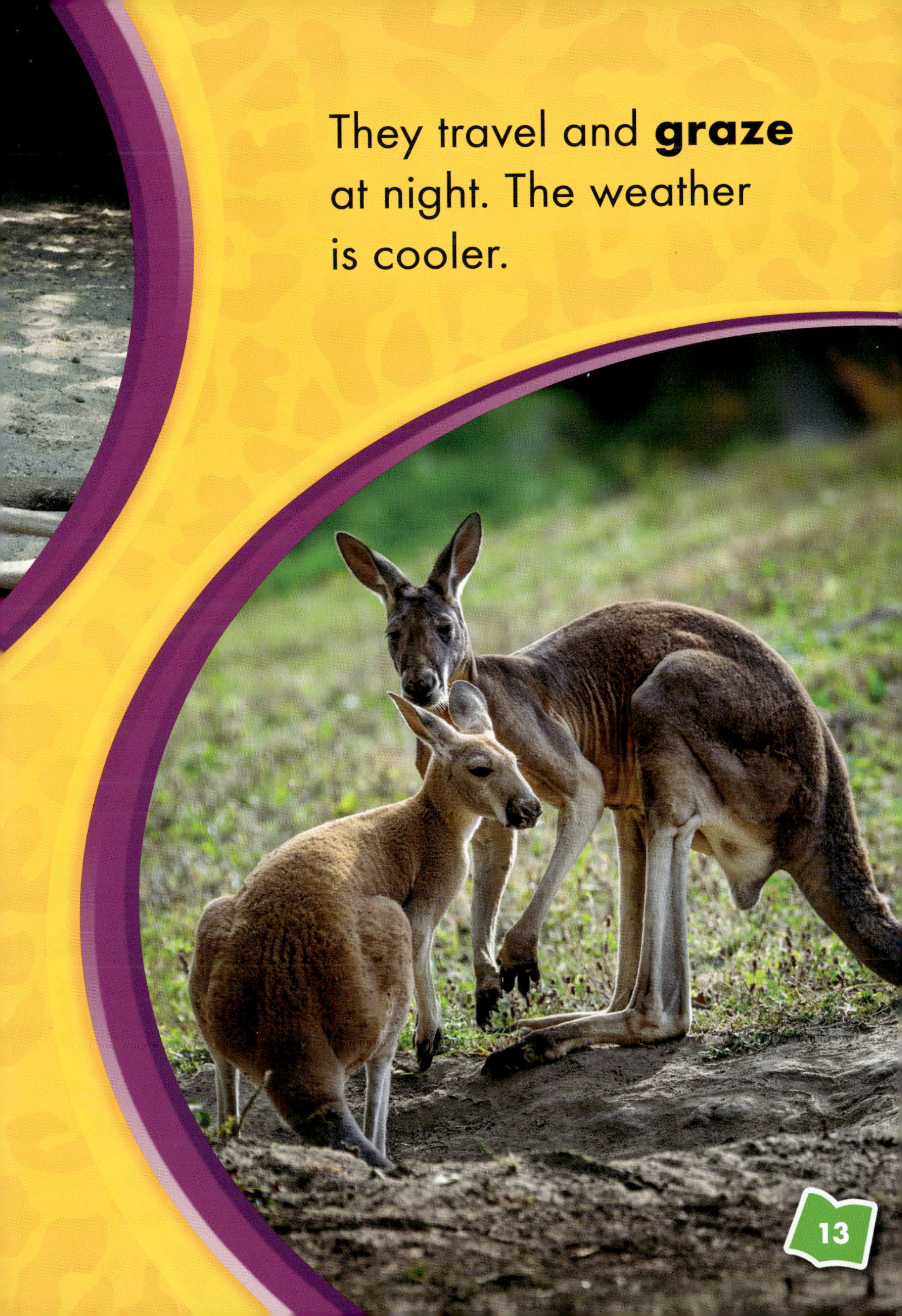

They travel and **graze** at night. The weather is cooler.

Kangaroos live in **mobs**. Some mobs have over 100 kangaroos!

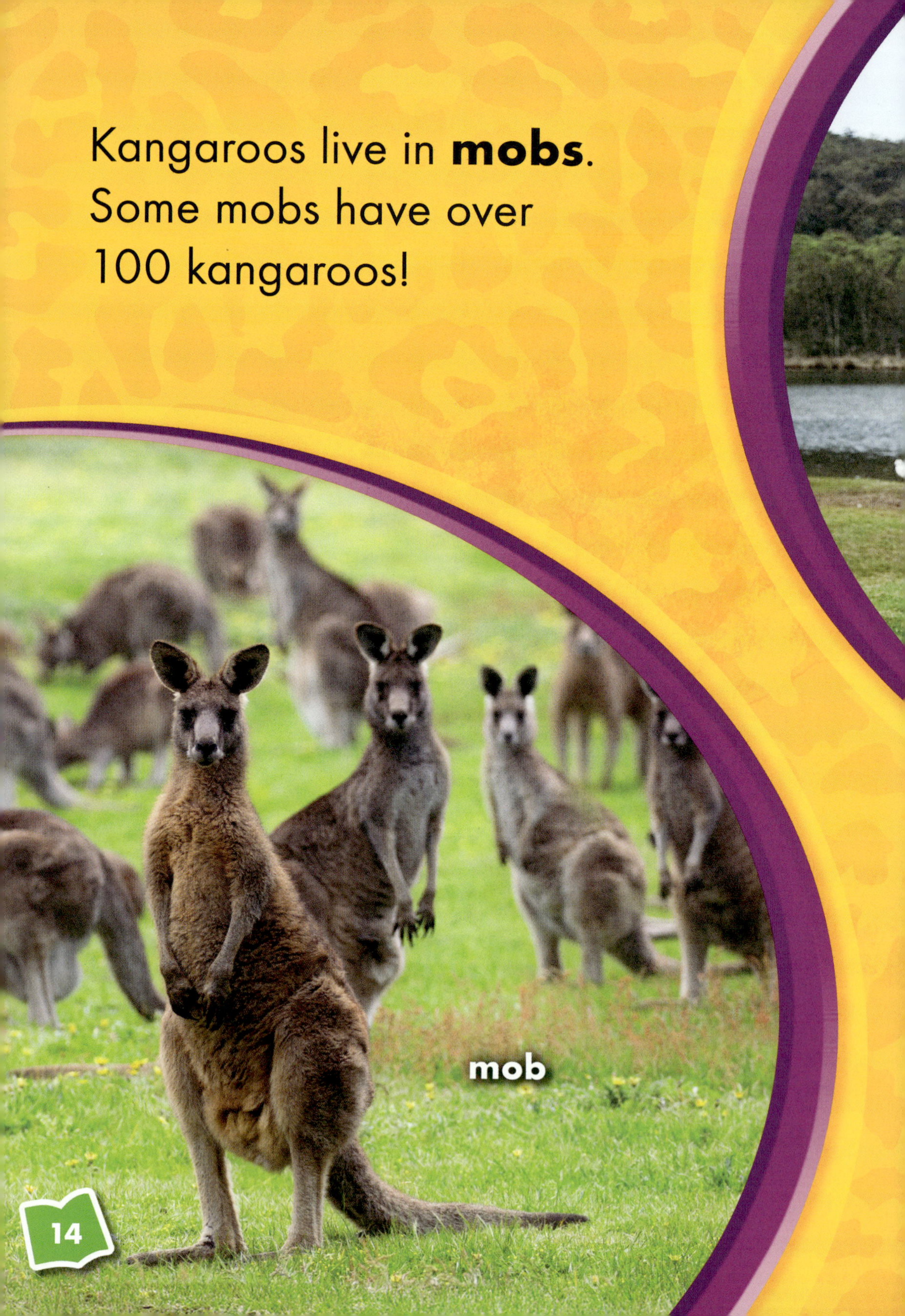

Mobs are led by **dominant** males. Males often **box** to lead mobs.

Kangaroos are **herbivores**. They eat grasses and shrubs. They get water from the plants they eat.

Kangaroos are hunted by dingoes. They kick and box dingoes to stay safe.

Growing Up

Female kangaroos give birth to one **joey** at a time.

Joeys are born without hair. They are tiny. They cannot see.

Joeys stay in mom's pouch as they grow.

Joeys stay with mom for around a year or more. They can live up to 23 years!

Glossary

balance—to stay upright

box—to hit or punch

deserts—dry lands with few plants and little rainfall

dominant—commanding or leading

graze—to eat grasses and other plants on the ground

herbivores—animals that only eat plants

joey—a baby kangaroo

marsupials—mammals that carry their young in pouches; mammals are warm-blooded animals that have backbones and feed their young milk.

mobs—groups of kangaroos

savannas—flat grasslands with few trees

To Learn More

AT THE LIBRARY

Anderson, Shannon. *Kangaroo*. Coral Springs, Fla.: Seahorse Publishing, 2023.

Duling, Kaitlyn. *Kangaroos*. Minneapolis, Minn.: Bellwether Media, 2021.

Sabelko, Rebecca. *Australia*. Minneapolis, Minn.: Bellwether Media, 2023.

ON THE WEB

FACTSURFER

Factsurfer.com gives you a safe, fun way to find more information.

1. Go to www.factsurfer.com.
2. Enter "kangaroos" into the search box and click .
3. Select your book cover to see a list of related content.

Index

box, 15, 17
claws, 10
ears, 10, 11
eat, 16
feet, 8, 10
herbivores, 16
joeys, 18, 20, 21
legs, 8, 11
marsupials, 4, 6
mobs, 14, 15
pouches, 4, 20
tails, 9, 11

The images in this book are reproduced through the courtesy of: GlobalP, front cover (kangaroo); anjahennern, front cover (background); Caseinfocus, pp. 2-3; Smileus, p. 3; Imogen Warren, p. 4; Picture Partners/ Alamy Stock Photo, p. 6; Laura Romin & Larry Dalton/ Alamy Stock Photo, p. 7; Westend61 GmbH/ Alamy Stock Photo, p. 8; Freder, p. 9; RudiErnst, p. 10; kyslynskahal, pp. 10-11; Natalia Fedosova, p. 11; nzld.photo, p. 12; Volodymyr Burdiak, p. 13; AscentXmedia, p. 14; Breathes, p. 15; Ingo Oeland/ Alamy Stock Photo, pp. 16-17, 21; Photography by Rob D, p. 17 (dingoes); Karen Brough, p. 17 (kangaroo); Mark Marathon/ Wikipedia, p. 17 (grasses); KarenHBlack, p. 17 (shrubs); Avalon.red/ Alamy Stock Photo, p. 18; imageBROKER.com GmbH & Co. KG/ Alamy Stock Photo, pp. 18-19; Damian Lugowski, p. 20; schankz, p. 23.